GEORGE WASHINGTON

Also by Adam Fitzgerald

THE LATE PARADE

GEORGE WASHINGTON

Poems

Adam Fitzgerald

Liveright Publishing Corporation
A Division of W. W. Norton & Company
Independent Publishers Since 1923
New York London

Printed in the United States of America
First Edition

For information about permission to reproduce selections from this book,
write to Permissions, Liveright Publishing Corporation,
a division of W. W. Norton & Company, Inc.,
500 Fifth Avenue, New York, NY 10110

For information about special discounts for bulk purchases, please contact
W. W. Norton Special Sales at specialsales@wwnorton.com or 800-233-4830

Manufacturing by Berryville Graphics
Book design by Lovedog Studio
Production manager: Julia Druskin

ISBN 978-1-63149-100-9

Liveright Publishing Corporation
500 Fifth Avenue, New York, N.Y. 10110
www.wwnorton.com

W. W. Norton & Company Ltd.
15 Carlisle Street, London W1D 3BS

1 2 3 4 5 6 7 8 9 0

CONTENTS

There are two Laundromats, the inevitable McDonald's,
a Howard Johnson, assorted discount leather outlets,
video arcades, a miniature golf course, two run-down
amusement parks, a fake fort where a real one once stood,
a Dairy-Mart, a Donut-land, and a four-star Ramada Inn
built over an ancient Indian burial ground.

—Susan Howe

GEORGE WASHINGTON

The Lordly Hudson

After my family died there was a replacement family.
I lost my dog but soon a replacement one arrived
in tassel bow the color of goose stuffing and liver.

My replacement house followed after the real one
was blown apart. A replacement head and tunic of
lilac and locust came in the mail for me soon after.

Later, replacement hands retrofitted my actual ones,
their lines resembling the rivers that span the district
where I was born between the replacement Garden

State Parkway and the Turnpike. Replacement light
and shadow congregate across the ceiling though
it's still the same old ceiling above my same old bed.

Blue replacement pelicans must be lovely to behold.
A replacement sun rises in the East and sometimes
sets softly like the smell of burning hair in the West.

In my former life, "The Lordly Hudson" was one
of my favorite poems, its serenade and arcane grandeur
somewhat inspiring then. Still, the replacement version

doesn't really do much for my brain's chronic
synaptic degradation. I own a banjo. It sits atop
the debris of my privileged life: socks, shoehorns,

erotic cassettes. No need one replacement afternoon
for nostalgia to fill my lungs but like mercury it does,
the way sleep singes our casual bodies at evening.

Nothing's missing yet sadness falls in me like something.
Replacement dad knows the pain, son. Replacement me
crawls to the fridge and opens the freezer door, its glow

enshrining my dumb face. About my replacement self,
I feel only average levels of attachment and revulsion,
inconsequence. One day you make love to a replacement

having finally bedded the person you loved. And before
long, replacement you lounges with replacement them
on a green sofa that is a fine forgery of itself. You could

barge in, copying and pasting random saws from heroes
but your voice would only mean your insides curdle to
nothing but birds. Replacement kids hoe bisexual gardens.

Replacement agents sprawl in saunas awaiting their spines
to flake into petunias, mulch and tendril, insect and screed.
And whoever you are probably just left a little while ago.

Oregon Trail

A thief stole 6 oxen from your wagon.

SPACE BAR to continue.

You decide to rest.

You lug back 88 lbs. of otter meat.

You have reached Blue River Crossing.

Bindi has died.

You have typhoid.

Next landmark: 88 miles.

You have exhaustion.

You have fish odor syndrome.

You lose 3 sets of relatives and 84 Sharpies.

Your supplies: 2 oxen, no clothing, 3 wagon wheels.

SPACE BAR to continue.

You find a turtle shell with no turtle in it.

You have herpes.

You have anthrax.

You have polyps.

The wagon tipped over while you were womanizing.

You have reached Blue River Crossing.

You have family trust issues.

You read "We who are parting."

Smoke-flowers blur red river.

You sleep late.

You have $90,000 in outstanding college loan debt.

The river flows alone.

SPACE BAR to continue.

Mountains are surly and blue-haired.

A cloud floats from its mark.

You gleam like birds.

Here lies Brad Pitt.

Here lies Raptor Jesus.

Microsoft Word does not recognize the name Shaniqua.

You have jaundice, congenital arthritis and calyx blisters.

You have no one.

You wail, holler, cry, screech and slam.

You are doable in a jiff, crunch, pinch or jot.

You marry Xanax to Flonase.

SPACE BAR to continue.

Your circadian rhythms are fucked.

You wonder what happens to tampons in airports.

You have engorged lipids.

You figure out the meaning of finger bowls.

You inherit *The Christian Science Monitor.*

The river flows alone.

Your mind goes away.

Everyone in our party has left for another party.

Would you like to look around?

Our Lady of South Dakota

Our Lady of Allen, South Dakota, be with us.
Our Lady of turquoise towers and water pumps,
of dry barbiturate skies barreling o'er granaries,
bucolic at the continental pole of inaccessibility.

Our Lady of Brundage and Wounded Knee,
pray for us. Average family income 2,300 USD.
Our Lady of Tagg Flats, think of us sometime.
In Elmo, Montana, in McNary, Arizona, near

Parmelee and Dunseith, steer our grubby tykes
through the promises of Sunday Pay-Per-View.
Our Lady of Boys Town, weep for us in aisles
bleaker than Walmarts in Belden and Muniz.

Shampooers and fast food fryers, nanny aides
and drivers work for greasy wads in zippered sheets
stained with love. Our Lady of Del Mar Heights,
what's the dillio? Lady of Calio, Madonna of

Oglala, Virgin of Las Lomas, Mother of Whiterocks
and Winslow West, scrunchies and lip gloss flake
about your departing feet. Glam metal, nourish us.
Roseanne reruns, comfort us. Prairie casinos, protect us.

I saw Our Lady in Spring Creek and North Hartwell,
in La Rosita and Nageezi, by Lago and Lukachukai
looking bedraggled about the eyes. Her wrinkles tied
in crow's-feet, bellied by refrigerated mac 'n' cheese,

hair-curler stiff, stinking of lye and Marlboro Reds,
cleaning ranch condominiums littered with coolers
of heavenly Coors Light. Our Lady of Sheep Springs
wrestling for Friendly's blintzes. Our yellow-lipped,

chubby-wristed mother, flowing in tie-dye muumuu,
cucumber sundress, pebble-fisted, softly skirting along
kiddie pools on unmown lawns in babyshit peep-toe
platforms, by handlebar streamers humping paydirt.

In Sawmill and La Puerta, bring Kool-Aid coupons
and save us our White Castle gallon-kind big slurps.
Give ever your grist to the grits of highway rest stops.
Our Lady of Wanblee, help rebuild the bleachers at

Butterfield Regional Middle School where the boys
grope their camera phones in shadow, zit-stippled,
molested by high-voltage power wires arching across
aluminum meadows, steel ladies tacking clotheslines.

Our Lady of Gentle Snowfall, Mudslides and Indoor
Home Plumbing. Our Lady of BuzzFeed and Tyler Perry.
Our Lady of Pooper Scoopers and Ketchup Dispensaries.
Our Lady of Skechers and Old Navy, of Dental Dams

and Grease Trucks, of Single Mothers and Closet Cases,
Road Rage and Outlets, of Trailer Parks and Cereal,
Our Lady of Monday Night Football, Our Lady All About
Consumer Confidence, RVs and Veterans—be with us now.

Blue Yodel No. 5

I was a mountain once
written by a blind hand
and there I stood remote
from human interference
just a mountain of stuff
not distinguished so much
lording over my domain
sovereign in neutral space
contained as I wanted or
inclement as I had to be
shape my distortion and
that wasn't really bad.
What rolled down my sides
flowed in my sound mind
left little sleep to reason.
Walk my barren clime.
Pitch wherever you like.
No longer part of nature,
scrub-weed fills my head.
When the grass was full
I sang a different song.

George Washington

You were my gym buddy ferreting along spotty fluorescent ramps.
Misbegotten signals blinked out bumpkin lanes over sable grass.

We passed through many things. Peach sirens, entryway orderlies.
Mangled disposition-stations. Chief in disbelief was concrete love.

Firmer still, a melee awkwardness that showed all registrants just
how we managed to pickpocket night. Then came dark crowds.

Some doodled for the pad, debriefed what pumiced eyes meant
in multi-dotted foreign rows. Buildings like a spider's clothes.

Later, we sped backwards. A maw orchard, windless in the mind,
boomed electronic lifts. I spied you at the prow of some sensation.

I declined to call another name. Pelting noise flew off fairy citadels.
Clocks, first thought abducted, were switched. Dialogues dispelled.

My love heard a mug crash on the countertop of Long Island Sound.
Our people became as ones lost. Not many rebounded with pledge,

not many fetched familiars, stretched legs, reread white meetings.
O stream, ring your ears. Handsome tubers, go ahead and wig out.

Modern territories click a mouse. Body becomes human body.
On skinny avenue I hushed up pyramidal steps older than sorcery.

You know how I want to share a dust-ball with misty partner.
Dance one fabled evening and hear the skylark do something.

Picnics bended over, they happen below. Swings parks rung.
I inject chlorine into my memory-parts with lady satisfaction.

Are you gay? A political campaign sanctioned a quart of moose.
So stars soon quarreled back to the travel section of the North.

Ignoring that, I opened my lips for a job to crunch and push
at me, seeing the flat spacey wherewithal of disconnected items.

I want a second act. What can I say but this was my second act.
Must wrangle a look-see. The sign revenging its timely laziness

in the ruffled strut of an accusing pillow. I hibernate in phrase
perfect as the mood of blue lotus stalks. Public aspects. The

last shipment of VHS tapes left its factory on this day in 2008
or 2009. Meanwhile, delis around town don't go like they used to.

Who cares if I can't hose down my you, my Newfoundland.
And George Washington, someone we can't really know, rows

over famed waters, wondering what his face will be, not in
the future, not for the monthly book-clubs, but as sovereign:

as beast with dunce cap. I will dress you down in fresh lettuce
and gobble your ear off with smutty keys principled as music.

The marching saints won't bother in battalion to much know.
We make of him so much hackneyed affection, dress wounds

as if equivocal all need. Hunger passes through the other side.
Entertaining pals you wouldn't call but couldn't not think to.

I don't know how he crossed the channels of that stout city.
One thing we share is worshipping the image of a person we never knew.

Prospero's Books

It's Nobody Beats the Wiz one day, closed for good the next.
Jesus sits there behind a dozen Picture-in-Picture displays.
Like the Wizard of Oz, you live for Red Dot Special coffee.
So Mary Martin plays Peter Pan and passes from the earth.

Shipmates in Nebuchadnezzar's beard were we one summer eve
by Dippy Octopus, Ali Baba and his forty teacups. Go with me.
The Hanging Gardens of Carmen Sandiego trouble our cable box.
No more *Casino* now, no Newport Lights, no Kent III Ultras.

My freak-out was like everyone's except mine included Gielgud
naked while ghost-men marched ruffled in the buff, ginger ale
pouring down the wax cheese passages of my skull. You step in
Grandpappy's steroidal creams, cairned to sleep in sofa-pit seats.

Goodbye, Blockbuster Video! Farewell to the Monopoly Man.
Read up on UFOs. Marvel at their beginnings: an interracial
Vermont couple sees aliens. We vacationed with JVC Camcorder
at CVS Euphrates. Delta Burke left *Designing Women* in 1991.

Leaves of Grass

[1]

The internet replaced stores owned by men in splotched overalls that once inspired Norman Rockwell in New Rochelle. There, Rockwell shared a studio with cartoonist Clyde Forsythe and submitted his first cover painting for *The Saturday Evening Post*, of which T. S. Eliot wrote in a letter dated October 1929: "With regard to the *Saturday Evening Post*, I shall be glad to consult a fellow-director who is better acquainted with American periodicals than I am, and will write to you again in a few days. I also have in mind *The Ladies Home Journal*, which published Mr Strachey's *Elizabeth and Essex*, and which is rather more than its name suggests, as a medium."

[2]

The Private Lives of Elizabeth and Essex was a 1939 Hollywood historical romance. It featured Bette Davis, Errol Flynn and Olivia de Havilland. Running just 106 minutes and made for a mere million dollars, it was produced by Warner Bros. Pictures. In 1986, the first Suncoast store opened in Roseville, Minnesota—stocking cassettes, LaserDisc, eventually DVD and Blu-ray formats. As a child, I frequented the interconnected suites of Challenge Arcade, Spencer Gifts, KB Toys, Roy Rogers, Ruby Tuesday, Pizzatella, Wok Express, Bun N'Burger.

[3]

In 1826, Samuel Lord founded Lord & Taylor on Catherine Street to sell hosiery, misses' wear, and imported cashmere shawls. Brooks Brothers has outfitted 39 of the 44 American presidents; FDR brandished a Brooks Brothers collared cape and fedora at Yalta in 1945. Between 1846 and 1848, construction began at 280 Broadway of the Marble Palace, or Sun Building—the flagship of the largest dry goods store in the world. Designed by Butler Snook, the original architect of the Grand Central Depot, he completed the project in 1871 only to see it torn down not two decades later to make way for Grand Central Terminal. The online directory for Grand Central Terminal includes the Apple Store, Banana Republic, Cobbler & Shine, Eddie's Shoe Repair, GNC Live Well, Kidding Around Toys, Leather Spa, LittleMissMatched, L'Occitane, Pylones, Tia's Place, Toto, Tumi and Vince Camuto.

[4]

In 1855, Walt Whitman published *Leaves of Grass*, writing these lines from section 12:

> *The butcher-boy puts off his killing-clothes, or sharpens his*
> *knife at the stall in the market,*
> *I loiter enjoying his repartee and his shuffle and break-down.*

Walt Whitman Shops formerly known as Walt Whitman Mall is a commercial center located in South Huntington, New York, on Route 110. The shopping plaza, just down the road from the poet's birthplace, is currently undergoing large-scale renovations. A statue in honor of the poet, along with new restrooms, automated doors as well as canopies for several bus stops on the south side of the mall, is forthcoming.

Low-Impact Fat-Burning Workout

How does one grow the cojones to celebrate a Fudgsicle?
I'll tell you, and won't begin by mentioning trellises forsooth.
The items on the register are mechanisms inscrutable, yes.
But they sway in the doubled-up air with a sense of lucidity,
A kind of gong affect that chiggers as it steamrolls forth,

Appraisals for unchintziest bling. Time for a sea change.
Your turn, and this means you
Come with me. Agreeable and mute, like the original
Doppelgänger, or as we in my neighborhood called it
The Doppler Radar.

On school mornings, a trust fund in my teeth,
High yacht vanilla swilled my parents' bed.
I would be multiple and exact.
From that vantage, a windpipe brought forth
On invisible horseback to the sick child's bed.

I'm sure you can't quite imagine it, ember
In the tabby lobby. But I could. I arrested it.
Gershwin and American Airlines and I could always
Tell the voice without the face, God's gift to me
For being lame in phlegmatic tissue. O parabola.

Look at the ashtrays! There they are. Swinging, roiling,
Ocean-choppy, a gauntlet of remote controls,
Paint supplies all stacked up with nowhere to go
In the corner of a grave illness—like pink paint.
This forecast of centenarians in Florida, and Burbank.

All my life I wanted a fractal tie and strawberry apron.
Now I'm a Church lady, no hint of arthritic condition.
My name isn't Sallie or Mae, it's Sallie Mae.
Millions of tiny pendants, Waterford crystal, bubbling
From local tree-fort where boys grope one another.

Will you come with me for Pilates at Fort Ticonderoga?
Denise Austin is here. Stretch in the sun.
Champagne woods, lakes chasms, dismounts.
Then you say: You have no idea what I lived through.
The Green Mountain Boys were like a second dad to me.

"Time After Time"

I'm in the barricade hearing the clock thickening you.
   Autumn encircles a confusion that's nothing new.
Flashback to warring eyes almost letting me drown.

Out of which, a picture of me walking in a foreign head.
   I can't hear what you said. Then you say: Cold room
(the second that life unwinds). A tinctured vase returns

to grass. Secrets doled out deep inside a drumbeat out
   of tune. Whatever you said was ghostly slow like
a second hand unwinding by match-light. Lying back

to the wheel, I shirked confusion. You already knew.
   Suitcases surround me. You picture me far ahead.
Yet I can't hear what you've said. You say: Doldrums,

have some secondhand wine. Love knew my precincts.
   The stone house turned black and the scenic tunics
were deep inside. Who said home? Oh, I fall behind.

That very secret height blinds. Lying like a diamond,
   the cock-thickening of you: hunchbacked arms, eyes
left behind. You'll picture me walking far, far ahead.

I hear what you've done. You said: Go slow. I feebly
   bleed out. Matthew's sermon turned out to be glass.
I wander in windows soft as Sour Patch. No rewind.

But something is out of touch and you're Sinbad.
   The second date was mine. In a private vacuum,
the thickening plot thinks of you. The future knew.

TOUCHDOWN. Lights. All those celebrity behinds.
   Suitcase full of weeds. You picture me coming to.
You: too close to me to hear what you've already said.

Then you say: The second wind unwinds. Doves whistle,
   halving their dovely backs, watching windows to see
if I'm okay. See it, the dulcet moment? I'm like thicket

tinkering for you. Fusion nothing new. Flashback to
   seagull-beguiled eyes. Sometimes talking to a barren
lad. Such music unbearably droll. The hand is mine.

Random picture-frames off the darkness. A Turing machine?
   Scotch-taping through windows, stolen from deep inside
rum-beaded thyme. You say also: Behind sequins & hinds . . .

And I'm in the barricade hearing the clock thickening you.
  Clematis enclosures, walking with news, pollinated by
a secondary grief while something reminds you of our love.

Big Data

Pharaonic Tarheel Bobbysoxers
cannot undo solace that comes
alone in accusative plural.
Plywood dentures ungulate
trinal outliers. Oceanic
sensibilities edify and expunge
crisp figments. Tracklayers
shuffle. Single-breasted punchers
examine malignant varicosity
as if babbitting exchange
scaled wheel-worn thud.
Deadlocked tubers, distal
vocality and clerkly hornbeak
grapnels deselect dismounts.
Ecclesiastes says, of one, crash
then caliph trug built back
to loopy racemes. Drownage
ports contrast; underbranch
circumclusions, liquid lunch,
plumcot funnels, apartments
gorgonian as sybaritic bubs.
Erlkings derby. Pigeonless
checkcards hyperchloric as
tailblocks intoxicate herds of

kale. Embody lake politics.
Packed trams spuke parliaments.
Arable tinselly vowers hive
after Ind. Dapifer spaniels
countermarch multipliable
notables round Muscovy glass.
Acknowledgers likened to
melodramatists, areole ruins,
botanologer readdressing fives,
dungforks scentifical by bilk.
Daintily, unlicking reigns
periplast rag-sotted face-to-face
meet and greets, porous
dockyard contact sports.
Attendancy almost Colossus.
Rosacea. Arrivance camphire.
Sustenation dietical. Linkboy
wavers. Tuberculosis precomposes
allotropicity. Squireen funicles
endorse dark-kerned airball
with graver linseed aloes.
Milksop engineers exercise
bonmot ricochets. Yankee
heeltools, semihistorical

verbarshadoof, fameless malar.
Annullers diddle subdeans,
embroideresses, flabile borders
cantillate trapstick guiltiness
akin to gasket relodgers.
Kickshaw emissaryship?
Bigamy superstratum?
Handwashing ministress
bimotors garboarded
gents of malicious plug.
Nonprescription cannery
wanders in a corf, its
lavic outtake—stulty
partners, extuberant
workmasters. Yes,
even some indecorous
sudoral glum.

How to Get Over Someone You Love

Begin by banishing the cymbal of a dream
locked in the retention of a nutrition label, go
to the echelon of what's remotely possible;
wear an escutcheon with meticulous scene
emblazoned in polymers that grant significance
to the microphones singers used in the forties
and the first daguerreotype of a Native American
to sit on a beveled Fifth Avenue mantelpiece.

Become more American. Study toll lanes
and how they open and close ponderously
in snowdrifts of upstate New York or appear
vertiginously on blue lumbering hills
along the Kentucky River—there's so much
baseball and white people rapping online
to distract from the beauty of a boarded window
that sits opposing you from lower vantage.

Finish the pixelated drawing you always
meant to conceive of in the back seat of a station
wagon as your ten-gallon hat collects dust
though there's a delicate frigate to draw upon
for inspiration as you urgently become lost
in a museum containing the last generation
of the LC2 computer—and didn't he make
an elegant bassist though the orchestra itself

was his principal instrument? The bathing
garments of childhood recover themselves
inside a second utopian community, eradicated
associationism compels skilled workers to
settle their differences with amoral stigma
linked to the constraints of ursine modes.
Just as in 3rd grade I was half-in and half-out
of a tub while *Little Women* was read to me.

Disown yourself of the slightest faith you
once held in crepuscular claims of hoaxes
and fabulist intricacies too bitter for tales
hyperrationalist in nature such as banal
medical testing performed on chimps and
baboons and shimmering artful reports
for trickster cosmetics older than columns
afforded to the wronged in *The New York Sun*.

Perhaps reconsider the shoulder bones of
buffalo or frank autobiographies indigenous
to brethren raised among petitions, tribal
disputes, public speeches, journey journals.
The Lord's Prayer might constitute similar
independence, the great noise of winterish
systems, even interior graphics spanning
revolts between Dakota Territory and Spain.

Close to the surface in most cases the prop
would bring you discovery doctrine, a court
for treatises and land purchase advocates,
the narratives rushed on horseback though
only a civilization like ours would doubt
the sadly applicable insight: we grow empty,
so the history of the disposed and irrelevant
consolidates into the solace of a second wife.

Militiamen are hunting after Black Hawk
in 1832 engaged in exactly this process
of entertainment, the process of shaping
circumscriptible offenses, the chill sunset
speaking for itself one single night over
the Pacific while a roofer whistles home
and the noble guests leave a room where
Metamora and *The Last of the Race* lie closed.

"That Thing Called Love" and "You
Can't Keep a Good Man Down" are only
two of my favorite Sophie Tucker records.
Thank you, February 14, 1920. A honky
studio band was believed to be involved.
A big soot tent and gowned wooden stage
are two of the most exemplary expedients
to demonstrate where people get their kicks

recoiling into a wilderness of feature and
gesture. And sharing with others through
the cork makeup and wigs of assertive
female singers, we can recompose two
things namely: 1/ that the wilderness of
daily experience is a dish best not served
outside parameters of fictionalization;
{ }

2/ the pleasure in error is something I
swear by, being itinerant, loving errancy
that way some boob straddles himself
in a crowded lift only to exit the first
floor that avails of cushy private space.
When you are well: complain, shrug.
When you feel death perfecting itself:
dance, compose, sing, thumb pianos.

The goal is to vilify consciousness as
overrated while by the same rebuking
movement to shuttle tenderly back its
reprieves, to notice the black liquor
bag not meant for casual consumption.
Rage has to enter the picture, preferably
from the foreground because it's already
present in ubiquitous facets of daily etc.

You don't want to guilelessly look up one
day and find yourself having completed
a Festschrift for a senior colleague without
having noticed the pattern in your research
as the Productivity Station background
flashes interminably. "Border Work, Border
Trouble"; "Divided Homes Not Homelands";
"Disenfranchised or Suburban Perversions?"

Welcome to the crucible of hours of envy
while you browse *The Cleveland Gazette*
and try to forget if Bert Williams or George
Walker are the determining foci of your life.
I'm sure I could tell you that hopeful degrees
and huge nostalgic faith will assuage that old
thing: the battering ram, some chain of mail,
the tacit view of power in classical sexuality.

I used to find the word *recovery* deliciously
loaded: its polite insistency that there was
a timeline of action, that raw sensation too
could be subjugated by sublime figuration.
The most common defects for high-yielding
success in the American vein is to displace
a social rise onto the repetitive and plain.
To pitch ordinariness back to wild wilds.

Would you like to come with me for some
old-fashioned inconclusive combat? Garble
a great deal of knowledge with Listerine.
But best to set out and disrupt the coding.
To grasp what Dewey means, think of some
of the ways in which we commonly seek
out significant experiences compensatorily.
The most profound internal mental stimulus

packages characterize our debate, divergent
funds and reckless humane proverbs of
questionable aesthetic integration—*anything*
not exactly the type of retribution today
that we should inquire of and dichotomize.
Yes, I know, it's lovely to live on a raft
a-gaze at speckled stars from broken backs
and have that quintessential homosocial

bonding experience in which we argue
whether they were all just made or rather
just happened as they're just too many.
Sometimes the river has allegorical contour.
Sometimes it's just a river in Westchester
you will happily never bother to discuss
again or for the first time if you're lucky.
Mystery, I suppose, is nature's accident.

Here's my accident: many of the ordered
properties that retain value to sense perception
after the memory has been enriched by
careful avoidance swing back ugly, unbidden.
And we might welcome them as openly
as we welcome the dissolution that wafts
from its suspended thurible so wantonly.
Thus, there is a sacrifice. But it's unknown.

And when the chosen organ of your will
is fondly amputated by a tenure committee,
to the motley substance of a stamp collection
you can withhold judgment and rush to join
water-control efforts in your local community.
A mariachi band isn't always corny delusion.
Some parish in New Orleans isn't pet project.
Drained and rebuilt, progress is a black-lace

shawl on which certain of us depend—
trappers, smugglers, Canadian *voyageurs*
plying with bottles of voluptuous interest.
The language of the future well may be
a pullulating glory of modern shipping trends.
My takeaway is to be stationed at the fringe
of a great emotional storm, to live it out,
but not forget along the way to live it out.

Here Comes the Hotstepper

Unlike my older brother, I generally enjoyed the nineties.
A world of Netscape, chat rooms and Fruit by the Foot.
I remember them like the debossed covers of R. L. Stein.
Neon sex toys dotting our suburban malls lead us to believe
in an intimacy communicated beyond brand names
when our couch sucked back into a shady hole of hands.
September came, laden with unused trapper keepers.
Macarenas were danced. Ring Pops were had. Giga Pets
and Beanie Babies, Dunkaroos and VHS cassettes.
The Little Golden Books by my bed told me stories.
Cedar Crest and chlorine. I remember snow days.
Watching humanoid Bob Barker on split-screen TV.
Closed armoires scented with piney Lemon Pledge.
In the woods was mesh and abandoned buckets of
porn beside inscrutable rainbow tree frog corpses.
Lisas and Jessicas and Matthews and Michaels all.
Narcotic and green, a risible lump disturbed life,
dizzying mallets hobbling us to plastic-farm noon.
Success metrics had incomparable swish. People
kept moving and threaded through one another
with slogging garage door jerkiness. And most
menacing: how happiness encroached with slow
ultimatums fatalistically stuck to stick-resistant pans.
Abundance, reversed now, feels shod. Feels pocked.

It could be no more than a rake in the trunk of a car.
I didn't know then what a locker room was for.
Friends were screen names and infinitely away.
If I had to point a finger, if I had to queue a song
to play my life, if the finishing move was finality,
wouldn't my sense of the nineties bring back painless
simplicity in transit? Weight Watchers and frozen
people. Linoleum not to be remembered if outlived.
Afterwards, I saw what they did to the bed furniture.
I knew their services weren't free. Not to "go there."
What was taken from me is still happening. Scrubbed
out. Tossed out. I never cared for the dishes. What
they replaced me with not me. That was never me.

RAS Syndrome

The La Brea Tar Pits literally means "the the tar tar pits."
River Avon and River Ouse both mean "river river"
even as Rillito River means "little river river" in Spanish,
as Mississippi River in Algonquian is "big river river."

Street Road passes through suburbs north of Philly.
Moorestown Township is a town in New Jersey.
Ai Weiwei was born in 1957. Yo-Yo Ma in 1955.
About Flavor Flav, JoJo Starbuck and Duran Duran

indubitably they are famous but surely no Snoop
Doggy Dogg, aka Snoop Dogg, aka Snoop Lion.
Chris Christie is an asshole and Kris Kristofferson
worked as a janitor at the *Blonde on Blonde* sessions.

William Carlos Williams went by Bill. Jar Jar Binks
was voiced by Ahmed Best. Tintin shouldn't be confused
with Rin Tin Tin, though this too I've perpetuated
my entire life. Woody Woodpecker is quite annoying.

The Eurasian lynx is *Lynx lynx*, the European otter *Lutra*
lutra, the South American coati *Nasua nasua*—all animals
classified by Carl Linnaeus, to whom most scholars also
attribute the origins of scientific racism. He described five

varieties of the human species in his works: the *Americanus*,
the *Europeanus*, the *Asiaticus*, the *Afer* or *Africanus* as well as
the *Monstrosus*—the latter for creatures such as the satyr,
the troglodyte, the hydra, Patagonian giant, the Dwarf of

the Alps. At night, before I submerge to sleep, I dream
of pitch-black darkness, of ATM machines that go idle
and wait for touch, the zillion PIN numbers activating
LCD displays. Beyond my dud garage are trees trimmed

carefully as poodle dogs. Down south, it rains. Big brawny
bodies trawl for tuna fish, seeking the actual facts of their
lived lives by lunar tides. When a particular item's found
it's déjà vu all over again. Roast beef with *au jus* sauce.

PowerPoint History of the VCR

Mr. Belvedere is there with Care Bears, cowering cherubs and obstructionist judges bearing Frosted Flakes by the bushel. Imagine gold porcelain across a skeletal body, some beefcake with popular boy's name ca. 1973. Your derby folks were parsimonious enough to pinch out Easter as we sit on beaches beneath gendered skies, the pyramids of a thousand empires falling. I cast myself as Holly Hunter. The burbs petrify, go ass-out on a cathode bed. Mavis Beacon teaches stereotyping and flips off birds. Las Vegas college weekend vacation party prom dress. You nympho bunk, get your 12-year-old creepy hairdo away from me. To occupy the right place. To punctuate breath without fault. Alice Deejay lisped to me in P.E. *I'm still bisexual* and for a second it's New Orleans all over again. Gallant as Nembutal, you came to me, a touch of circus aphasia and collagen, such soft-serve eyes. Put a dick in an aperitif. What have you? Snapple Corp doesn't give two shits. But the blue river of youth, impervious to change yet changing nonetheless, a mini-mall minimalism mind, reminds you of heroics, adult film dervishes. I padded conscience o'er with duffle jeans of dapifer crystal. Under Consuelo's arches, a paddy bun comes. And you, you gurgle rubber anthems with kitchen-sink English. Like hoof glue we go. I'm sorry. July died in a tragic pole vaulting accident. In his casket? Barney. Magnetic tape holds together the top three networks' tiered rating systems, lavish first-run palaces, revenues totaling 17 billion. Hi. I know 90 characters of Pi.

First-Person Shooter

I outlaw all forms of nature.
I commit intrigue for calibrators.
I short shrift on gummy rafts.
I expunge permanent records.
I consign tomorrow to fiefdoms.
I rinse myself with chthonic immensities.
I treat fan mail like death threats.
I upchuck missionaries.
I loathe those who loathe meat.
I follow Court TV.
I slump in spandex on a patio.
I feel post-gender at the moment.
I join a regional intramural drum circle.
I ballyhoo and curtsy. I take Sudafed.
I whack off. I go numb. I go boom.
I pull my test scores way up.
I contain immortal lodgings.
I recommend a nice therapist to a friend.
I stockpile thank-you cards.
I talk like an escalator going backwards.
I accept my charm's facile quality.
I believe in Jesus. I miss you. I miss the point.
I torture who you tell me to.
I repel tension with immaculate spelling.

I should keep my mouth in a gun lobby.
I absolve you in fire, finish you with cuneiform.
I swashbuckle Listerine. I chew Trident. I plug a new book.
I marry a spigot named Heloise. I retire to dry docks. I spew.
I hype. I bust. I have the type of music playing in my lungs you like.
I do cameos on European soaps. I sit like a fly on a piece of wax fruit.
I sleep in the shower, fuck in the dark, make for quick study.
I have a herniated bachelor living in my backyard.
I tuck into offshoots.
I sniff burbled offal.
I celebrate gay eulogies.
I grind brass in quandaries.
I play the flute.
I say a bunch of shit without thinking.
I form a demolition league.
I gurgle, giggle, collect debt.
I think of the good times.
I live in Newfoundland.

Riverboat

[1]

So hard to know which shape you're supposed to breathe with. Or that's what you say to yourself in the trappings of a clock closet with stained windows of no exact economical epoch. They have a charm unto themselves like grandsires boarding a riverboat, gambling with fated history, its sedentary grammars, unforgiving marshes, broad and encroaching yet devoid of descriptive as smokestacks replenish the sky—with passengers coming in and out of focus, nothing too erratic about them, tired as we all are, or at least I am. Think of it another way: the toy deck of a bottled ship reflected in the wayward eyes of some nightingale. There's really little room to imagine someone affixing names to all the infinitesimal passengers who'll never squeeze upon the thimble-sized ship. What garments worn, what passions stowed or tucked like so, what the weather said to those for whom it was their final passage. The riverboat turns panoramic, a monolithic set-piece, superbly two-dimensional, varnished by day labor, brighter than the most fastidious railings out on the open seas in the heyday of industry. It sits, awkward, a relative whose name we can't place, who smiles in contrast to the boredom of the hour. Grubby shoulders lean against the stolid frame of its tenuous design. Meanwhile, no one sees the billboard-big barge, especially those with benign intention, gleeful surging nuptials.

[2]

The idea of the riverboat has size, so in immaculate prefabricated halls with great many windows and unsurprisingly artificial light, a student maps the last cusp and ventricle of its proportions, the wavelength hulk of its anterior, the impacted cube of its cargo. A panel convenes. Some argue about the wisdom inherent in the suppositions of "the idea of the riverboat." Namely, whether any idea cannot *not* be infinite, which is to say, precisely, not that the idea of it need be without space but that it necessarily might surpass time: an exponentially expandable phenomena. Samuel Clemens does or does not have a mustache. Whether or not he has precisely 31,000 days left on this planet at the time of the maiden ship's venturing forth, there remains an infinite number of ships complete with slightest variations adrift on quantum foam throughout eternity. Perhaps they're there in the sound-shape "ship" and whether or not activated they still must be brought about. If so, only then does the river not become immeasurable duration.

[3]

The riverboat could be actual. A writer on assignment might be on it. Whether an authentic, nautically correct, seaworthy vessel is neither here nor there; aboard the ship that isn't yet disclosed. Dreaming upon said riverboat, the image assumes valences of all sorts of family dramas, missed connections, perhaps the fragrant wrinkles of an irreplaceable palm. Experience animates and underwrites it. Memory colors it. Her stern undersides abide. Not that the riverboat has to be especially meaningful, desirable, but, in Tucson tonight, part of a person dies and the huge cogwheel that turns and churns on muddy water performs an unanticipated dance, stoically alone, quite possibly heroic. The dream writes itself onto a set of arbitrary realities that will always be more precious than whatever we elect to think or suppose we feel about the passing gallant belle. Like a giant child's fan, oversized and plain, an emblem of the Age of Wooden Seas, she paddles on the clear materializing waters. Into the warp and woof of the riverside's sedge the lurking hull purchases rest, and one day, the ship's retirement will have nothing ritualistic about it. The boat idles, rusts, lodges into the landscape's wharf as it disassembles, reemerging every so often: keychain, penknife, slogan or theme park. *Water Gamblers*, *River People*, *Inside the Pirate South.* Producer last name Stevedore.

[4]

No one wants to mention riverboats, hear of them, read any
more academically sanctioned monographs distilling their
Americanized ingenuity. Moratorium has been placed on the
name. It will no longer appear in this poem. Some will miss it
as others begin the next close-to-but-not-quite craze, inventions
of sexier, more profitable matter. Tales of spinning jennies,
parachutes, steamships, human hauls bandied about the board
room, amidst school cafeterias, all-night diners, neon motels.
People in your home district read this, as does your local
assemblyman. So too others in slums and on yachts, with kidneys
in transit, persons of interest, select members atop high-rise
luncheons. Sea shanties weep. College freshman re-enroll in
Introductory Spinoza. Bitches be flippin' and somewhere, in
gargantuan eaves with hickory-limbed bayou, around the mouth
of a harbor, with entirely benign though somewhat mediocre
starlight out in force amain, the trees whoosh and sough, tides
primeval await, and she, unpeopled now, but noble in her
plodding self-sanctioned task, rolls lugubriously, majestically
onwards, to her appointed rounds.

Product Placement

Make orders have been transmitted.
Ports and distances will be crossed.
Nimble digits screw on my head.
My torso is like a song of silicon.
Against the surface of a thousand floors
I am tested and ready to depart.
Screaming faxes guarantee arrival.
Dials are knuckled by important VPs.
Toll booth operators are standing by
across continents. Logs contain
pixelated command strings. I am
shipped. Tools of the toolmakers
have been used on me. The million
beads of voided sweat fugitively fall.
Chemists and model-casters have
cut me down to size. Pressure gauges
allay fears of transit packaging.
Tiny geometrics plot the drive.
Carrier vans come for cardboard.
I clatter at large unloading docks
in the ermine density of morning.
Ingenious forklifts bury me in hulls.
Sweetly jammed into a simulacra,
mildewed docking gates fly open.

Rudder struts applied are tightening.
Cargos push off to sea like crayons
in a bathtub. Deadbolts drop in buckets.
Hangar bays seal my fate like manic
Disney teacups carving curvy lanes.
Roadie radios facilitate my insurance.
Purchased policies don't deny me.
Carpets sterilize; coffeemakers bristle.
Satellite spunk relays my coordinates.
Vendors clock their rushed dispersals.
Tongues become hatches hatching.
Repairs swing into being after toupees
are combed, conference calls had, board
rooms waylaid, legal pads jotted on.
Rest assured, nothing's happening.
Winds move. Circuit boards braid
micro-guts that manage the tides of
stars, a teeming sense of definition.
Lovely human forms steer my travails.
Cleaning fluid sits in bulk beside me.
Christmas morns await. Windshields
stationed at the edge of Ohio creeks
scratch the deep belly of Nebraska plains.
Crystal points establish. Data inevitable.

Clanging horns shatter Gibraltar rocks.
Yoda Toyotas. Dehumidifiers. And I am
locked up, set loose, patrolled laterally,
gauged, shuffled, blinking, hauled off.
Near a Denny's in Nevada, you'll find me.
Batting rackets know my name. Nothing
richer than the rich ubiquity of plastics.
Everything has been crushed exactly right.
Bags of antenna parts. Toy walkie-talkies.
Like skin cream, I am of good use to you
along the conveyor belt of the Pacific,
the trillion lbs. of me pouring out, saying
only, only, only that my love is yours.

Ocean of Dick

Questions remain about the sexuality of the historical Jesus.
Across abandoned lawns in South Detroit, kids chuck rocks.
Over text one day, they says to the other: "Follow me."

*

Imagine a sleepy college town on the northeast. Iffy hetero
guys. Arguments about nostalgia in early gangsta rap. Talks on
Catherine Opie, Kohl's, the hacker revolution.

*

Senator Nebuchadnezzar (R-NV) had dreams in the second
year of his term and couldn't sleep. Thoughts of night-visions,
thickening dumb sleep. Like a sword in your ribs.

*

My subconscious wars even as my physical maleness remains,
like a chemical weapon, to suppress and explore. Like a sea of
persons, rhythmic and integrated, Light from Light, true God
from true God, begotten not made.

*

And entering the sepulcher, they saw a young man clothed in
white; and they suffered great panic. And he said, Be not afraid.
He is risen; he is not here. Behold the place where they laid him.

*

Words drop from me like rubber snakes. I pull the sponge of so many pale, dark flowers to my mouth, around my neck, sleeved into my thighs. Imagine them piled in heaps and heaps. Like the dead: gentle and limp.

White Noise

THIS IS WHERE THE SERPENT HIDES
WHITE ELECTION NERF GUN USA
SUPER SOAKERS BY THE BUTTLOADS
DEADLOCK AT ENEMY'S BASE
POWER RANGERS FEED-A-THON
MT DEW DANK IN THE MOUTH
DEADLY COCKSPANIEL HEDGES
TRENCHCOATS ICE CUBES SUCK
CUTOUTS WACKY KHAKIS YES PLZ
HAVE YOU SEEN IT HIS SHOTGUN
GLASS ANT FARM THE MIGHTY
LIGHT POLLUTION OUTBACK STEAK
HOUSE WHITE WATER RAFTING
FROM A FAMILY OF UNCLES
PISSY FREELOADERS MI AMIGA ES
SU AMIGA W/LEGWARMERS WE GO
WITH GARAGE OPENERS WITH
BRAIN-CRUD BONGS HOSTAGE
NEGOTIATION SITUATIONS LEAD
OFF HIT NEW SUNDAY BLUES
GYM CLUBS WEAK CHIN WEAK
SAUCE FISTFUL OF POTATO SALAD
WHAT'S ON THE DOCKET 4 DIN
DIN SPRADDLE MY PADDLE CALL

AUNT SALLY I LIKE WHERE THIS
IS GOING TRY MY ABBLASTER
MENACE IS A SILENT CREEPING
SICKNESS CEREAL NOT FUNNY
SHINGLES 4 THE HOLIDAYS FREE
REBATES CUSTODY LAWN DARTS
TAKE OUT THE TRASH OUT 4
LIFE 4 PRESIDENT PURPLE STUFF
SUNNY D KINDA PRETTY FAGGY
POLAR BEAR THANKSGIVINGS
SORRY TERRIBLE DIDN'T KNOW
PLEASE FETUS THE LINE LEADER
IS IT OKAY TO ASK QUESTIONS
ALL IS FINE NO PROBLEMO R.I.P.
TOOTHFAIRY HONEY MUSTARD
PINK BRINK OF INTELLIGIBILITY
MUST SATIFSY WHOOPING COUGH
ACTIVE SHOOTER TRAINING ROLL
OUT MENU ASH HEAP GUTTERS
FORTRESS BUTTER BOAT GRAVY
PAINTRAIN CLAPONCLAPOFF THE
CLAPPER I CAN'T GET UP THE SUN
SHINES ON MAZDA MIATA ASSFACED
SILLY PUTTY CAPTAIN BARF FACE

DIVORCE DAD JUST A LAWN YOU
MOW IT DREW RYAN JORDAN
MAX JAKE CONNOR DICKWAD JR
PLAY ME PLAY WITH ME PLAY BY
PLAY PAY-TO-PLAY FLIP CUP PHONE
FUCK PEANUT ROCKED STOCKED
LOADED LOVE TETANUS WATCH
OUT 4 STINK EYE WHIZ KID MATH
GENIUS MANCAVE BACHELOR PAD
BIG DOG MUSCLES PIZZA PARTY
SPIDER PLANTS GONE COMMANDO
BARN DOOR OPEN HANG OUT
HANGMAN COME WATCH STUFF
TOTAL PERV ONLINE AIM ATM
PEGGY ANN MCKAY BUMMER
KNOCKED UP OFF MIKE TYSON'S
BOXING BEST VIDEO GAME EVER
SHOPPER'S ADVANTAGE PLUS BAG
CHEEZ-ITS TAPIOCA PUDDING
IMMUNIZATION SHOTS GLOCK
MOCK3 STADIUM DRESSING GOWN
SALAD DEVELOPMENT ETERNAL
HOURS WISDOM TEETH NOFUCKSGIVEN
BABYJESUS REEBOK WHAT A KICKER

Dead Girls

White people prefer murder
To happen to strangers
Viewers prefer stories about dead girls
Though drowning is popular
Beachfronts are popular
Houses by the bay
Houses by the lake
Bodies of water have a long-studied relationship to suddenly passing away
The scene is a chemistry classroom
Daylight's undertaker makeup
My boyfriend sullen and cute
There are flashbacks
To dancing designer drugs
Inside bloated McMansions
Where deodorant commercials play on loop
The detective learns how he hit me
How I wore his lost necklace
How my BFF made out with aliens
My life a mystery
Everyone hungry
The fate of my name on the lips of the curious
Our coach encouraged me
My dad bloated with grief
My breasts small

My pelvis slight
My blue corpse is angular in daylight
Multiple autopsies are performed
Murder sleeps in our midst
A princess from Connecticut
In the middle of life taken
Under the covers of psychiatry
But no one tells anything
When they find my body
Floating through the marsh
My mother ghosts the room
Worn to a stony nub
The season is almost over
Blood calls to blood
The mayor and governor convene
Nothing can stop until the Waterfront Project's completed
In my life, are you the happy girl or am I?
In the story of my life, do you mind not knowing?

Eternal September

Abraham begat Isaac who begat "Percy's Song," *Hook*, the Bride of Calvary, Ralph Waldo Emerson and SimCity 2000, Edwin Arlington Robinson, Book VI of the *Aeneid*, Ulysses and "blood chubby," Araby, Bazarov, *Jacob*'s *Room*, Memphis Minnie and the Carter Family, Big Bill Broonzy, Blind Lemon, Blind Willie and Elizabeth Cotten, *The Decline of the West*, Nietzsche, Plato, Lysis, Hephaestus and TMZ, Cy Twombly, Leona Helmsley, Laurel and Hardy, Johnny Rapid and Jimmy Durante, Octavio Paz, Samuel Greenberg, Al Jolson, the Book of Revelations, Sir Thomas Browne and *On Being Blue*, Robert Burton, *A Death in Jerusalem*, *The Apostle*, Saint Anthony and "tripping balls," West Cork, Sam and Flan, Dingbats, Wingdings, Linotype, the First Folio and *I'll Drown My Book*, Algiers, *The Telephone Book*, Georges Perec, *Life* magazine and Chuck E. Cheese, Gambit, *Jurassic Park*, Lando Calrissian, the Phantasm, Catwoman, Mr. Freeze and Bell Atlantic, Toys "R" Us, Rosalind Krauss, Gomer Pyle, PBS, Maurice Blanchot and Andrei Bely, Clarice Lispector, Clarice Starling, Inspector Javert, Edmund Waller, *The Kiss*, *The Falls* and Granite Ware Oval Roaster, Joan Murray, Ruth Herschberger, *The Trauma of Everyday Life*, Bob Jones University and Wagga Wagga, Albert Einstein, Niels Bohr, Paul Dirac, Marie Curie, the Nobel Committee, University of Paris and Erwin Planck, the Gestapo, PalmPilot, Google Reader, Flash, Napster, chat rooms, Richard Milhous Nixon, April 22, 1994.

1776

Into impossible zones
smoke scarves, naturally

terrified itch bespoken by the stop-gap
the stop-gap's ear

it was another city there
buoyed towers hung down
not so low
        as you

weddings, each time of year
Easter deer at red grove

but before this
an utterance—

the puckered radish of Tuscaloosa

had a car, drove many miles
some many miles before
it driving itself, wild mechanical ducks
patch-tent

resting at Yard Inn
the fence snakes a bit, wraps around melted mountains
like a handshake ago
questions of blue ox

meet me by it

both irregular the nocturnal shunt—
neo-adjuvant they watch
themselves recently former, not past

pixelated cone people

he stepped to the plate
with mercurial finery
and goose sense

in the invariant inclement however
stark lot/items

a book opens, morning
the story rote—who were we where
we were (about it)

the end
drifters drift, planetary in their passing

weighted scales, volleys
middling barns
de-vestments

each fragmentary nation
a nation

each bale, hoof, cusp, pin
enough

herringed folks
mopping the block

while the rotation
receives swerve
black "receipts"

—is this it
—would you like it to be

to prefer the dense stoicism of
night's anti-terrestrial crank
a kind that doesn't exist

but OK

I want things concrete, things in a green box
lake in the window, smoking rubbish fire
you just tables and tables, and plenty
ruptured—

no
the story of a white road (run off)

do you mean by that you're hung up
somewhere

invariance—

The mute chalk clock
handling passengers—

and *1776*, my sci-fi romance

we need orchestration, parking lots, new ones
no

astro-pain, astro-light, astro-sleep

                    sleep

Vader in Love

[1]

Start by assuming the ideological ramifications of imperialism as seen through its cultural, as in artistic, offspring; the differences between culture and empire, between colonialism and imperialism, are keen. So too, their sense inscribed within a totally foreign systematic logic, the process of the artwork, its making and maker, even then, further off to the periphery, the slightly odious bunks and house-squats referred to as biographical context, the interior life, the soil of which man is the intelligence, not just of what transacts and is experienced, discarded or immolated through imaginative expiation, but rather what in being transformed, remains still unapologetically there, lodged, not fully absorbed by the mental body. The human body but the idea of the mind, said Spinoza. Though one thinks of the lag between source material and product in tons of creative endeavors—the way *ex nihilo* is a spongy dream chock-full of coral reef-like structures, cavernous entry points, persistently personal preoccupations so that the reader might regard the pungency buried in a turning phrase to reveal all sorts of prismatic light. Shaded over by dingy lusts, mood lighting, lava lamps, "this business of dicks & cunts." Tabloids sour easily, fold their linings in the bowels of yesterday's vast techno-capital expediency. News that stays forgotten, sufficient unto no tomorrow.

[2]

Sitting on the toilet, fingering some crisp Vintage paperback, the idea occurs to me quite naturally, moribund as it is. That the fashion that was Western studies is like an allegory unwritten down of not just makers making—how quaint (repellent)—but of one body falling in love with another. The wrong one. The narrator at the end of *Swann in Love*: "I'm in love with a woman who doesn't even appeal to me." But the French, says S, says J, registers closer to the general vicinity of "who wasn't even my type" and I hear the phrase pushing itself idiomatically further, perversely, to "not really my kind of thing." There are centers and peripheries to desire. Material appropriated from one place, unconsciously smuggled in backdoors of exacting association. Our feeling-animal states find inside another, for the time being, a geographic site, enacted on the portholes of the senses, through couches and canals of raw experience: a tattoo needle at the spine. I steal a line from radio static. Paganini rebounds with dippy violins across thematic centuries. Hayden Christensen plays Darth Vader né Skywalker marching to cloying blue-screen sound-tracked by John Williams who went to the same Los Angeles high school as Susan Sontag. Mahler: funeral marches; Williams: daffy trumpeting. Culture plays tug-of-war inside the best of Mahler's symphonies: mazurkas, folk dances, kiddie choirs, polka ballyhoo. How do all these things gel in a canonical 20th-century sense of things? I'm rushing into the arms of an inanimate lover the way Emily Dickinson says she rushed into the arms of a cold: kisses and caresses about her nape. Pedantry, ideas, rhetoric, sophistry: mental junkspace that "Philosophy don't know." In *Glittering Images*, Camille Paglia pronounces George Lucas the great artist of our age.

[3]

There are powers in a phrase of music—a musical phrase of poetry—that make me feel like Dak in *The Empire Strikes Back*, ready to take on the whole thing myself. The elation and elevation of certain sentence sounds, patterned vowels and sibilants. Like it's summer and I want to be wanted more than anything else in the world. *I shall be King and you shall be Queen.* In the imperial centers that concentrically make up self, there are instants when AP Euro flashes upon tensile pond scum the way Caesar had a hard-on for the Rhine. His Latinate instruction, proud; that firm declension set to go off like a landmine inside the LEGO block forests of the German language. Later, they recombine and England, now and forever, lurches free. If pedantry's a defense mechanism in poetry, is desire something like that too, in terms of intimacy, of address, of bodies? "Gesture": a very German-sounding word. Geist, ghost, gestalt. To the Roman Empire, German Idealism's one answer. Pornography, another. My fantasy life: lit-up with uncomfortable spiels, blocked questers. Are you the type of person who sees sex as the means to transcendence or transcendence itself? V. S. Naipaul interviewed in the *NYRB*. Meanwhile Vader's in love again. Queer figure. Broadway Wagner. The dark side as narcissistic embrace, machismo's paroxysm. Hiccups, rashes, boils, break outs, burnt splotches, dark patches, spots of time. Hollywood Manichaeism. *Antony and Cleopatra*: the same ancient hangup of public vs. private selves alive in callow Aeneas, dialogue courtesy of ghost-writer Tom Stoppard. Libidinal machinery when it comes to human facial tissue fascinates me. In the headless bureaucracy of empire a sprawling constellation of influences. Noun: Tunisia. Noun: 20th Century Fox Inc. Pringles. Conspicuous consumption. Cultural capital. Geo-monopoly.

[4]

Myself: mad King George pursuing thirteen colonies. And yet I doubt a laureled viceroy sits above the map and plucks his toys too willfully. World War military history suggests differently. Mahler's Tenth: incomplete, his last, posthumously played. Recorded, century later torrented. My silver sense: disked anonymous waves. Diaphanous fabric, dapple-freckled. Huge black velvet backdrop pinned with sequins. What you call stars. Metaphor, the conquistador's. It upends and suspends, appropriates and consumes, for transference to achieve its thing so the mind confirms/conforms whatever eidolon it holds like a refuge moon above the salient woods of Endor. We shall be given the word for everything: industry, trade, law, journalism, politics, religion from Cape Horn clear to Surith's Sound. Romantic Love but a 19th-century holdover, a fair amount of rollover minutes on this plan's calling card. So I call, I plan, despair, text, swig violets, leave. *A Leave-Taking.* One day in history, I read the line "We were taken to the ice prison, a palace encrusted with hoarfrost, its dome lit from within . . ." But in my mind I remember only "ice palace." *Mansfield Park*, *Heart of Darkness*, *Aida*. Stories of empire and tales of love, Said dared to say. So I write love's privilege. Ruined marble feet flanking Appian Way. The giant toe of night, cosmetically sealed off to tourists, lies naked for cameras come day. Kitten postcards in the ankle crevice of a statue c/o "What at night had been perfect and ideal was by day the more or less defective real." O Night: desiring, imperious. "The hydroelectric plant is not built into the Rhine River as was the old wooden bridge that joined bank with bank for hundreds of years. Rather the river is dammed up into the power plant. What the river is now, namely, a water power supplier, derives from out of the essence of the power station."

[5]

In love we all have ports of call, social ranks and trade channels, bondholders and promotions, governmental attitudes and isles for consensus, unconditional creativity. Dayton, Ohio Peace Summits. Departmental views to the contrary, a letter is sent at evening but the note never comes to the allegorical windowsill. Much like the way that landscape enjoins sky, language abuts the ash of unspoken others. There are images: fleece, fax, books on Braille at discount. The "you" of the poem like night and day—all moony with special ambience, dispatched by busying banality. By early afternoon? Ambien. Trawling the Cloisters. Rush to the embroidered boudoir of your plaited hair. Like Orlando, time matters not to me. Nor woman neither. The dumb roles don't have to be scripted nor dubbed later because we have a garment of cauliflower to feel tender about adjacent to sensations of bootlace and flax. The dream of all empires is the end of time. What's a poem? A crystal bay by which the lights of passing ships blink on, off. Innocuous cattails and fantails presented luxurious to touch. My boy like lady waiting under Queen-Anne's-something. O sad boy of lovely shadows. What I feel for you is bound calfskin of antiquated knowledge. It evaporates, litigates, the spur and spar of unused credit. There are many confections to seize: his metal cravat as burnished helmet cockscrews on with pressurized suck. His meticulous leather gloves gripping obviously human-actor hands. The love of father and son that is sometimes metaphorically the love of man for younger man, master for apprentice. Still, the shot that means the most to me happens in the elevated catwalk among darkened trees screened in by seventies concrete décor. His back to the screen, on a railing he turns away—one patient scuba-diver's audible bubble of pause—and says: *It is too late for me, my son.*

To New Jersey

Certainly not the state with the prettiest name.
Even so, your once metastasizing malls and lots,
your vegetable kingdoms and finicky, punctuated
sky of pale pollutions, hold some attention still.

Long Island: a pancreas whose bilious head is BK.
You: a kidney, compacted graffiti of the letter S,
whose veiny highways, turnpikes, gibbering tunnels
yield yet the city's trash some passage home.

Meanwhile, a confiscated hockey puck lives lodged
along your white cul-de-sacs' prefabricated mores.
Avocado sedans, boardwalks and bulwarks, Metroid
and Mega Man surface—a sweet debris that rusts

your summery prewar factories. Like soft tubes of
denture adhesive or avuncular railings atop spindly
ozone trucks, you stay. With catalectic rivers, gouty
topless shores, swooping shadows' stapled masonry

you fold your hard-flecked, boiling Chrysler clouds
into the grace of these deranged department stores
and chaste used dealerships, traumatic concrete skies.
Few pills more pretty than your shabby sofa lawns.

Freeway Raceway opens. Freeway Raceway closes.
Woodbridge, Quakerbridge, Willowbrook open.
Woodbridge, Quakerbridge, Willowbrook close.
Yet inside you're something that can't be destroyed.

Slimy stolid parts slither through your airy creases
while your lemon skull ricochets alien brain patter.
Plastic Dixie knives wiggle in your Jell-O organs,
your hazard parking cone lungs where valets bend

your labile ducts as ominous as tummy tucks
forming the scar of a single Dorito dangling down.
Pool clubs like little ruffled tracheas. Your onion
moat DMVs, your bifurcated yoga mats and sprigs

from heather woods lacquering Sugar Wafer lakes.
Around olios of Gemzar jazz, oozy colic aftershaves,
tongue-pantone shades, tender salmon pediatrics,
the slop and chafe of your ciliated blocks all white

and brown and black through endless warehouses,
microwavable pancakes, dump sites, Ghosts 'n Goblins
lost inside jolly funeral homes, chuffy radiation stuff
from your burnt, loving side voluptuously flows.

Elegy in a Courtyard Marriott

Palookaville, no more! Do you know what we did
with the beach balls? Never had them. But
swimmies represented achievement in water breathing.
Much like on turkey day, when floats lard the sky
and a tumorous squirt gun orients us home.

You make a metaphor of tan lines, garble grunge
in garages where cobwebs nest and fizzle,
leaves of diplomas straightening helmeted snow.
The day ends by doctored dickering, corn puffs.
Blankets of soon and almost there.

The real world's over. What's left are inalienable alloys,
whiffing slippers, a society of doughnut fins that flutter
around kiddie wheels espying germ hoods.
Gassy roses that underlie the existential sense
that in the grand motel lobby of life, cum cars come.

If you could sing a little in my pants, we'd come back
to the splintering point, take our slogan summer to its origin,
a myth of Verizon and greeting cards, days of our lives.
Inescapable trial, celebrity murder. Your
theory squiggles like a liver aloft, experiential, vectoring.

What my green scum says is mute. Consummate paranoia.
But the lectern is brick, and we toss it—they die—
one at a time, a Danube of bureaus, lady parts, no nuts.
Butter mounds of pancakes on the earth. So a
family finds entertainment—among prolix warning labels,

malformed neurons, the fat queen mattress of a burned-down
house. What difference does the white light make
humming in the house when shades drawn, death final.
What difference these seascapes that trim whitecaps.
I hold your hands the way a wig sleeps at night.

Happiness Machines

The lawn grows into toppled flamingos and bowling balls.
Only yesterday you were telling me about hometown psychology.

It must feel thirsty to float in the infinite expanse of outer space.
So many years and generations have passed since this poem began.

Little Jacob has grown up, operates a boom mic on the weekends.
Every other month, he goes with cousin to skate park, what's left

of it. We sweat and lean over a concrete pool. Kick things in it.
I sense there's a lot left in me to be discovered, flipping through

brochures for adopting pets, watching reunions with mannequins.
In bed at night, I watch documentaries on Sudoku, wonder what

happened to aerosol spray cans. I could go for crab cakes at a diner
in Roselle Park. What's the weight of an idea? Does it fluctuate

between half-uttered thoughts in the limbic system? You died.
Edward Bernays, the nephew of Freud, invented public relations.

The Remake

Jurassic Park comes back
Star Wars comes back
The Clintons and Bushes come back
But you do not come back
The Terminator comes back
Teenage Mutant Ninja Turtles comes back
Game Boys and Payless
Billy Graham and Mike Tyson
They all come back
Romeo perches on a tomb
Exiting the perfume of his grave
Little Orphan Annie
Tina Turner inside the Thunderdome
Kenny Chesney's "I Go Back"
YouTube girl singing "Back to Black"
Coleco and tanning salons
9th graders popping E
They all come back
But you do not come back
Godzilla lumbers out of the ocean
From a preserve of nuclear debris
Princess Diana appears over Egypt
Bathed in a shawl of landmines
Pee-wee's Playhouse

Thomas the Tank Engine
Syndicated reruns
Reunions and specials
All come roaring back
Polio returns to Newark
Inside the eyes of Grover
Cleveland Alexander
LL Cool J comes back
Bill Nye the Science Guy comes back
Total Recall comes back
St. Joseph's Aspirin comes back
The MGM Lion lies down with Lamb Chop
Choker necklaces and fanny packs
Amos 'n' Andy and Doc Martens
They all come back
The consumer revolution riots eternal spring
Twinkies and Polaroids
Hatchbacks and Wendy's
Federal bombings and OJ
Cancer clusters and *The Mummy*
In the golden age of returns
Resurrections are replayed
From the feral gardens of my brain
Betamax and Norwalk viruses

Bruce Wayne and Bruce Lee
Into an assembly hall they go
Lavender and termites
Breakfast mints and green screens
They all come back
Goosebumps and wrestling
From a fold in the earth
Outpouring of ground
We welcome them
Without you
While on the glint of a dime
The rigid nose of our 33rd President
Is alive and well

Final Boss

These are Bowser's breeding grounds. A lost and found in Hackensack, NJ.
Save and Save As come out and tutor me their gay minimalisms on the web.
Penicillin sorbet calls from the refuse of a development plaza. Here where

Buffalo Bill first had physical, where Fascism for Yuppies started support group
and Atlantis went deep dish, doling catheters out for the carpool drive home.
No cyanide grass grows, no medicinal aftertaste. And the final boss approaches.

Spillway alligators sing freshmen anthems. Sausage cufflinks rotisserie carpets.
My corpse: a pulse of midland space sixpacked up & ready to go. Sorry, Gumby,
for a silly death. Like Kelsey Grammer at DoubleTree, I hammer amid clouds.

The princess is scorched and scotched, tenderly radiated and missing in action.
After the proper names left me, mostly nowhere felt right save the cancers and
xenophobic hate of Our Father wrapped in Saran wrap, while drugs poured in

and ethnicity was bleached out, Drano style. What remained was a ghost tense.
A world of colonial homes, opal grass. Turtled mountains cleaned by Electrolux.
The truth is I didn't mind so much, not knowing the delicate barking wasn't for

me, that clams weren't historical wallets. I didn't mind what happened to anyone,
save for squid-white menace exploding in a billion pipes over 2D chlorine seas.
The taste and trace of you, my final boss. After a thousand years, I fell asleep.

Poem with Accidental Memory

That we go back to life one day, the next,
Some other century where we were alive,

When music spelled itself out to us, often
Incomplete, and nothing was more vague

Than the banality of whom to love and lose
In line, the doppelgängers in rimless snow,

Or even now, in summer, at day, by night,
When something oblivious, replete, turns

Back at us in idolatrous quiet, so we see
Who in nullified particulars we really are

At a desk of our own making, filling in for
Someone else's life sentence, blots drying

On a silk tie having no meaning but today's,
When the loner puts his insomnia to rest.

George Washington

I don't remember exactly when I wrote "George Washington"
I'm sure it was in the spring of 2013 traveling
Greyhound upstate to visit Joe and his newborn.
The poem flowed haphazardly then, breaking down
the page in random lines. After a few months' time
it slowly boiled over, the fat hissing into couplets.
I lived on 7th Street between 1st and 2nd then.

I remember wanting to write "George Washington" earlier,
one inspiration the night Geoffrey and Simone
and Ariana came over to my place while it rained
more than it had the entire summer. Ariana said how
she'd wanted to title a poem "George Washington Slept Here."
My unconscious must have filed that fitfully away
yet often I have no idea why poems or titles

prompt themselves with certain irrepressible urgings
years later. Perhaps I wrote the poem recalling
the time when viral videos first became a thing:
Washington, Washington, six-foot-eight weighs a fucking ton,
opponents beware, he's coming, he's coming . . . etc.
I hated that video. YouTube launched somewhere
in San Mateo, CA—2006?—I can't be sure when.

I see *George Washington* was uploaded January 2008,
the year I moved back to Boston. I'd left in 2005.
Still, I can't remember either period that well.
My family's house burned down that February
the same one I resumed smoking after someone
I'd been long-distance dating decided to end things
by seeing their on/off-again boyfriend once again

claiming they'd both live together in Miami or
Las Vegas. I can't recall which tacky city. I met him
in Binghamton as well, like my friend Joe, who I was
coming from when I wrote "George Washington."
When my book came out Joe brought me up
a few months later. There I'd meet another boy
from Binghamton whom later I had convinced

"George Washington" was written just for him
though I did edit in "Long Island" after meeting him.
I see now I must've written it in April. The bus
wasn't Greyhound. That so few of the particulars
in my mind aren't interchangeable somehow proves
poetry is memory. Have you read "George Washington"?
It was published in *Poetry* with two other poems.

One written after my dad died, the other for some boy.
Poetry is a kind of nullity. For a long time, I thought
I'd call my next book *George Washington* so I began
reading a bio about him, pretty unknowable guy.
I typed up applications with "forthcoming collection
entitled *George Washington*" saying things like: "I see
this spontaneous subject matter represented something

internal and personal through the guise of an aloof
father figure. The Founding Father, in fact. One
reader cued me to something more abstract: 'Americana,'
its symbols transformed through 21st-century idioms.
From Whitman and the Mississippi to shopping malls
and the inhuman quantum physics of the internet.
Part of what I've been exploring is how estranging

these ubiquitous, half-forgotten tokens are today."
I went months and years not speaking to the boys
I've been referring to but they resurface sometimes.
What's a poem like without a single metaphor in it?
Out of this combination of aloneness and experience,
I guess: the nervous creations I identify chiefly with.
Are you willing to ride with me to the time I wrote

"George Washington," speed ahead with me to when
(last September) I got things in shape I mean my
poem. Lines fell away. I wonder how long I'll live,
how the rest will be like, I mean the rest of the poem.
On Wikipedia I look up stuff about photography.
I learn that *hyperfocal distance* is the length beyond
which objects turn sharp, lens focused at infinity.

Grief and desire are just two of the key themes in
"George Washington"; both bend upon unknowing
as when you learn more about George Washington
you see his teeth weren't wood but pulled from slaves—
that sentiment betrays as soon as it brings anything into
acceptable focus. That doesn't bode too well for
knowing either. Grief: knowing. Desire: unknowing.

And both—midnight uprisals that I know only too well.
I'm not sure now which the elegy, which the love poem,
but I'd still like my focus to be a type of distance I suppose.

ACKNOWLEDGMENTS

My gratitude to the editors of the following magazines and journals in which versions of these poems first appeared, sometimes in altered form: *The American Poetry Review*, *The American Scholar*, *BOMB* magazine, *Boston College Magazine*, *Boston Review*, *Granta*, *Hyperallergic*, *Lana Turner*, *The New Republic*, *The New Yorker*, *The Philadelphia Review of Books*, *Poetry*, *PostRoad* and *Prelude*.

Many thanks also to all the friends and colleagues who supported me in the creation and shaping of this book—especially Bob Weil, Will Menaker, Phil Marino, Peter Miller, Charlotte Sheedy, Deborah Landau, Anna Maron, Claudia Rankine, Timothy Donnelly, Cathy Park Hong, Dorothea Lasky, Kate Zambreno, Samantha Zighelboim, Nicholas Nace, Adam Phillips, Colm Tóibín, Eileen Myles, Kevin Killian, Ben Lerner, Robert Polito, John Ashbery, David Kermani, Emily Skillings and Dylan Furcall, my mom and brother.

ABOUT THE AUTHOR

Adam Fitzgerald is the previous author of *The Late Parade* (W. W. Norton / Liveright) and contributing editor for Literary Hub. He received his Master's in Editorial Studies at Boston University in 2008 and his Master of Fine Arts at Columbia University in 2011. He teaches creative writing at Rutgers University and New York University. He organizes The Home School (www.thehomeschool.org), a biannual poetry & arts conference for poets of all ages held in Hudson, New York and elsewhere. You can find him at *georgewashingtongeorgewashington.com*. He lives in New York City.